LIVING BENEATH

A Journey to Remember Between a Daughter and Her Mother

———— ✿ ————

by

Sonya Franklin Burney, Ed.D

Moving In My Gifts, LLC

Sonya Franklin Burney. © 2019

ISBN: 978-0-578-47053-5
Editors: P31 Publishing, LLC

Because of the dynamic nature of the internet, any web addresses or links contained in this book may have changed since publication and may no longer be valid. The views expressed in this work are solely those of the author and do not necessarily reflect the views of the publisher, and the publisher disclaims any responsibility for them.

Printed in the United States of America

Dedication

This book is dedicated to my grandmother, my mother, and all those who find themselves on the journey of being their loved one's "keeper." No one should live beneath love, forgiveness or their dignity.

Purpose

The first purpose of this book is to open up a much needed conversation in all families and communities about the unexpected journey of what happens when someone you know and love is diagnosed with dementia leading to Alzheimer's disease. From what I have seen and walked in my own journey, there is not enough communication about what this disease does to the patient and his or her family members and relationships. There is not enough discussion about how to handle the business affairs of the patient fairly and firmly. There must be discussion in all communities, whether African American, Latino, Asian, Caucasian communities, and so forth, including our churches, schools, social networkings, fraternities and sororities. There must be discussions rooted in love, forgiveness, and follow-through in order to survive.

The second purpose of this book is purely and selfishly a cathartic process for me (and my family) in watching one of the most brilliant women that I know, my mother, deal with the diagnosis and the realism of dementia in her life. Readers will also see the "unique" relationship that my mother and I have and how it plays into our relationship over the years. This is a process of understanding and forgiveness. This book also shares thoughts, emotions and yes--mistakes. I am not a medical doctor, but I want to share how the twists and turns of the progression of this disease can take its toll when you are unprepared.

The third purpose is to do whatever we can do to fight. So even though this is a heavy subject with heavy consequences, I choose to focus on the healing power of "shake your head" laughter from some poignant moments. I always try to draw the positive or laughter from the situation to keep it healing and moving.

On this journey, prayerfully a caregiver can come to terms with this disease over time through God's eyes, love and forgiveness. I will not forget the words of my grandmother as a young child when she said, **"Everyday, don't you forget when you wake up to thank God for a right mind and new day of life."** She was right. I hope that my story will be of help to someone. My name is Dr. Sonya Franklin Burney, and I am...Moving In My Gifts.

Table of Contents

Acknowledgments

You can try to live without God, but I cannot. I owe Him praise, worship and honor to all that has been good in my life; as well as what He has allowed to happen in my life to shape and mold me into who I am today. He reveals answers to my questions through His Word, praise and worship time, prayer, and people. He has never forsaken me. I know this may seem like a lot, but I know the challenges and battles that I have survived. So therefore, I do not take the credit for what He has done for me and those whom I love.

The Alzheimer's Association is totally awesome. I have visited their offices in my current state. But if you will take advantage of their services, you will find either in person or by phone, compassionate and caring people who want to help you and your loved one on this journey. Please find out where your local Alzheimer's Association office is in your own city. You will not regret it. They are absolute rockstars!

To my loving and supportive husband, Jerome Burney, thank you for being a true soldier. He chooses everyday to love me and our children. I am inspired by my family members in the great state of Michigan and my extended family members and cherished friends around the United States. My family and friends have always been one of my strengths.

Thank you to my mother and father for doing your best. God can take whatever we have and make it more than enough. You both reared me with godly expectations to live fearlessly and for this, I thank you. To my family and friends who chose to invest in me with their friendship and love, you have sown into good and fertile ground. I thank you for being obedient in moving to the call of God's voice. One thing that I do know for sure is that you will reap bountifully for trusting me with your relationships in more ways than you know.

Introduction

Dementia. At the mentioning of the name, my body is overcome with flashes of anger, pity, and a host of other feelings that are too numerous to explain. Unless you, or a family member have walked this path, no one has any idea what it means to become victim to, or caregiver of, a dementia patient. This crippling disease turns a capable person that you may love into a mere shell of who God created them to be. It is robbery. They are robbed of their short term memory and left open to be a victim to dangerous situations or people if no one is there to protect them. It is cruel to watch and endure, and at times can shake your faith in humanity. That capable person is held hostage inside of a failing body and memory that has betrayed its victim.

As a child, I was reared around a lot of senior citizens in my family, yet I can't remember a time when dementia-related disorders were so prevalent in society as they are today. Perhaps it was always around? Perhaps there was no diagnosis or name for it? From time to time, I would hear on television shows or movies of older folks "losing their minds," but nothing like it is today. I don't know what is to blame, but something has happened with nature, our quality of life, our food and our medicines. Health conditions are chronic and never seem to get "cured," just maintained over periods of time until leading to eventual death. This is unacceptable.

As I get older, I have seen the evidence of stress-induced lifestyles on many levels play a big role in the diagnosis of my mother's dementia. My mother was a great educator, and she lived by wanting to do everything perfectly. There is no such thing as perfection. This is too much pressure and stress to live under. We should do our best to live in excellence and move on. Different stressors such as her demanding and overwhelming career that she so loved, in return, did not love her back. Later on, the stress of being a caregiver in addition to the stress of dealing with the stress of her home and relationships were also considered as a part of her diagnosis. It is so important that we don't become busy with being "busy" and forget about what is healthy for the individual.

This is my story as a granddaughter, and now daughter of strong capable women who have lived with this disease. I chose to write about it so that it can bring more attention and awareness to so many that feel ashamed, or feel like they can't talk about it.

If you have experiences with this disease, I encourage you to share your story. We don't talk about this enough and how it impacts lives and relationships. I have learned that every person has their own story and no one has the power to take that from them. It is my pathway and I know what, and how I feel on this journey. I encourage you to tell your own story regarding dementia/Alzheimer's diseases because we need more stories that deal with this subject matter. Dementia, as with many diseases, also brings those truthful conversations and sometimes difficult decisions about handling business affairs and matters of the heart. It is my hope that this will help someone else become free of judgment, guilt, condemnation or anything else that would prevent them from making those hard decisions, or having candid conversations to protect themselves and their loved ones affected by dementia with Alzheimer changes.

Picture of Alzheimer's Brain Disease Progression

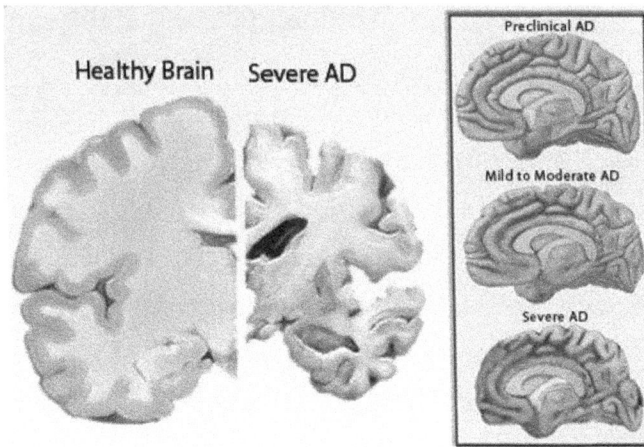

Portion 1: Healthy Brain/Severe AD: This portion of the photo shows the difference in the brain tissue of a healthy brain without Alzheimer's Disease versus the brain tissue that has been severely affected by Alzheimer's Disease. The healthy brain tissue looks full, while the severely affected tissue looks to have a shrunken appearance.

Portion 2: PreClinical AD, Mild to Moderate AD, Severe AD: The second portion of the photo shows the progression of what happens to the brain when affected with Alzheimer's. Over time, the brain tissue is affected by the disease and seems to "change" the brain and leaves adverse effects on the patient and his or her life. (https://www.medicinenet.com/image-collection/alzheimers_disease_picture/picture.htm)

Roles

My mother, who I call lovingly "Mom." Fierce mother, sister, daughter, and at one-time, a wife to my dad for almost 30 years. Prolific retired school principal. Caregiver and servant to my grandmother and grandfather; Dynamic Diva that will not be debilitated by dementia. She is left unnamed in the story because this story is relatable to many.

Dad—my loving father, who is awesome; my parents are divorced but they remain friends and are cordial.

"Mother"–Grandmother and my Grandfather "Gramps" —my maternal grandparents; matriarch and patriarch to the blessed family of 6 children, grandparents and great-grandparents to many offspring.

Narrator—The author, who is left unnamed in this story. This is my story, but there are many similarities and commonalities to my story that are shared in many families. I am the eldest child and only daughter of my mother.

Lenny—the enabled brother of the narrator; middle child of my mom and dad's three children; older brother to Marcus; struggles with alcohol.

Marcus-the baby brother of the narrator now married with a wife and beautiful family

Jeremiah-boyfriend who turned into awesome husband of the narrator

William—the eldest child of narrator's four children

Neurologist—diagnosed the dementia and gave a clear definition of the disease and cause

Chapter One

Three Powerful Words

Sunday afternoon in Ann Arbor, Michigan. It's late fall in 1991 and I hate that it gets dark at 4:00 in the afternoon. I hate this weather. Give me the beach, flip flops and warm weather any day. But for now, it's freshman year and I need to get my weekly check in call to my mom before she gets upset. I look at the phone on the wall inside my dorm room and strut over to dial the house phone number.

My mother answered the phone on the very first ring, which was different. She usually let it ring at least 2 or 3 times. The only time I have seen her do that is when my brother Lenny calls the house. It's like she has a radar or something and just knows it's him on the other line.

She answers very quietly, "Hello?"

"Mom you ok? You sound like you were taking a nap," I asked.

"No, I was waiting for your weekly call. How was school this week?"

"It was fine. How is everyone there?" You know the same old, same old. Nothing new. Well, since my Sunday night lineup of shows was about to come on, I needed to get this wrapped up.

"Ok, well Mom, I have to go and study for a test but I will call you again next week, ok?"

Mom answers quietly, "Ok…" and her voice trails off.

"Are you sure you are alright, Mom? Where is Dad, because you don't sound right."

Then all of a sudden, she pipes up her voice and says in her most happiest of tones:

"I love you!" and before I could react or respond---she hung up on me! *What? What did she say? Did she say what I thought she just said? Naahhhh! No way!* My mom has never told me that she loved me. So here I am standing in my dorm room wearing sweats, and my hair is half-combed at the age of 18 years old, and now she wants to tell me this? I had to move away from home to get her to tell me that she loved me? It couldn't be during high school graduation? What about after one of my many singing performances? Ok---wait--let me call her back. I think I must have misheard her.

I push the dial tone button and re-dial the home line again. She picks up on the second ring this time.

"Hello?" she answers.

"Mom, what did you say before you hung up on me?"

"You heard me. I said...I love you!"

"Oh, you *meant* to say that? Wow, ok." I was dumbfounded and speechless. This was weird. And then all of a sudden, I felt a little sad that it did feel weird. Maybe she told me this when I was born, but not anymore after that did she tell me that I could remember. Not when I started my first day in school in first grade, not when I had my first solo at church, not when I greeted both my baby brothers in the hospital as their big sister, not when I hit the major birthdays, went away twice for summer camp, or graduated from high school; my first remembrance was at the age of 18 as a freshman at the University of Michigan! I didn't know quite how to react. I didn't say, "I love you" back because I thought all of these years, she didn't love me. I just figured that was her. She had her way of loving me, but could never bring herself to utter the words with meaning to my face. Even when I said them to her first.

So for the next few Sundays, I would do my usual Sunday night call and she would say "I love you" at the end and quickly hang up before I could respond.

Then one Sunday evening as we are finishing the conversation, I was getting ready for the usual when she says,

"Ok babe, have a great week. I'll talk to you soon... I love you..."

She didn't hang up! She is still on the phone and waiting on me to respond!

"Mom, I love you too. And I will talk to you next week, ok?" I felt so awkward. I felt so embarrassed that I had to get into the rhythm of telling my mother, those 3 little words that make such a very big impact. As we both hung up, I stood there in awkward silence wondering what had just happened.

...So allow me to explain...

I didn't have the typical warm mother and daughter loving relationship as most mothers and daughters did. My mother didn't spend a lot of time fawning over my hair or talking to me about boys, or my changing body, or any of those mother daughter subjects. I knew of other girls who had these conversations regularly and I silently wished that we had them, too.

This was very confusing as a young girl trying to find her way and her niche in the world. It definitely played a part on my self-esteem, value, self-worth and how I viewed relationships. I would see her hug and kiss on my younger brothers right in front of me, but...never me. Even when I would ask for it, and she would just smile and pat me on the shoulder and walk away. I felt the sting and the brunt of it. At the time, I thought she meant it, but it would take years of unraveling to figure this out. My mother was demanding and hard to live with, and probably like most teenage kids, I found it hard to like my mother. She could be distant and aloof sometimes. I saw the difference that she made between me and my brothers. But, still as her child, I wanted her approval, her acceptance, and her love. I felt at times that she did love me when she made both of my prom dresses by hand, or would take me shopping for new shoes and a dress for Easter Sunday at church. I would also feel her love when we would leave from choir rehearsal at church and harmonize together while singing church songs in the car on the way home. I used to think that the reason why she made difference with me versus the other boys was because maybe she was disappointed that her first child wasn't the boy that she had always planned. That honor went to my brother, Lenny, the one she favored and fawned over simply because he was a boy.

I often thought to myself that when I grew up, I would never be like her. I would do everything the opposite. I didn't like my mother because I found her hard to understand. We were total opposites. She was an introvert, I was an extrovert. I showed my emotions and made sure that people knew full well what I was thinking, whereas, she wouldn't remark one way or the other. I have spent most of my life trying to reach my mother, instead of her trying to reach for me. I learned early on that I couldn't have that much needed acknowledgment of love. I had my father's love and was a daddy's girl--hands down! But unfortunately, I needed that validation. When children don't receive their validation at home, they will go looking for it elsewhere. Secondly, I always would remember those times of pain when I felt rejected by my mother.

Therefore, I can say that I have kept that promise. My own children have heard the words, "I love you," from the moment that they were born, in good times and in times of discipline and redirection. The impact of those three short powerful words, "I Love You," goes a long way in the development of a child through their adulthood and the choices they make for their lives. They should never be taken for granted. Say them and say them often. Believe me, having once been a child, who is now an adult raising her own children, I never get tired of hearing or saying these *three powerful words.*

Chapter Two

My Mother's First Love

My mother's first love is work. I mean she *loooooves* to work. She has the hands of her father, my maternal grandfather, who was also a hard worker, too. My mother, like most women, had a plan as to how her life should be but it may not have involved the typical marriage and kids. I think my mother was career-driven. She loved to work. I think she liked working more than she liked being married or raising children. But I think I do understand it better as I get older.

My mother is brilliant, very perceptive, and has a gift of discernment. She could "read" people and their intentions better than anyone that I knew. She was a perfectionist, which got on my nerves at home. I guess she missed that lesson in Sunday School when they taught that Jesus is the only perfect One that ever walked the earth. So, she did everything with perfection outside of the house. There was no denying promotions from her. Haters tried to hate, but guess what? You could not stop her from succeeding. I guess when she found her way, and things began to click,

she found her niche, her joy, her passion, her acceptance...
her love. This love was important to her because she felt
overlooked by her parents, her siblings, or any past people
who either broke her heart, or disappointed her expectations. She was excellent in all that she did on the job and no
one could deny her. She also didn't have to worry about so
much of a drain of her energy and time. She excelled and
she could...breathe. Did I like it at the time? No. But, I do
now understand.

Even my grandparents questioned how much she
worked. I will never forget the time when my grandparents
had come to town to visit one of my grandmother's sisters.
It was on a Friday night and the house smelled of popcorn
because we had all overdosed on popcorn waiting on my
mother to get home so we could go to dinner together. My
Dad had been home since 3pm that afternoon and had fallen
asleep in the den on the couch where the TV was watching
him. My grandparents arrived by 5pm from Ohio. We were
all home from school, me and my two brothers, and my dad
and now my grandparents from a road trip. My mom usually wouldn't get home until at least 6 or 7 pm, even though
school got out at 3 o'clock each day.

"Hey there!" said my grandparents warmly with hugs
and kisses as we greeted them at the door.

"Hi Mother! Hi Gramps!" Our grandparents were like
gold to us and we loved them! Our grandfather would give

us money and liked to eat candy, so we *really* liked him the most!

My Dad came down from upstairs and greeted my grandparents and asked my dad,

"Where is Penny?"

Dad said, "I tried to call the office phone but no answer, so I hope she is on her way."

My grandmother asked sharply, "What do you mean on her way? From where? Do you mean she has been at work all this time?" She was in disbelief.

"Yes, she does this a lot. I've tried to tell her that work is not going anywhere," as he shrugged his shoulders.

My grandfather shook his head and walked into the den to watch TV. We followed him to get the money and the candy. I think he knew this was going to take awhile.

My grandmother told my dad, "I'm going to talk to her about this because she can't do this every night. She has a family!" She let out a sigh and sat at the kitchen table and read a magazine while she waited.

I thought: *Yep! That's telling her Mother! I agree!*

My grandparents timed their trip when we could all go and eat dinner early and then have a nice and relaxing night at home. They couldn't believe that on a Friday night, she was coming home that late. When the clock turned to

7pm and I heard the familiar engine come up the driveway, I knew that Mom was home. When she came in the door, my grandmother was waiting for her when she walked in. *Showdown!*

My grandmother asked me if that was my mother's car coming into the garage.

I nodded my head yes and remained silent. I knew she wasn't angry with my mother, but I also knew my grandmother meant business and she had every intention of being heard.

"Hi, Mother!" my mother exclaims as she walks in the sidedoor. They exchange a quick hug.

"Well, hello, but don't you know what time it is?" asked my grandmother with a curious tone.

"Yes, I'm sorry I was trying to leave work, but there's so much to do..." as my mother's voice trails off, I almost started to feel sorry for her. I was witnessing my mother getting a "talking to" from her own mother. I felt guilty about it, even though it wasn't my doing or my fault. But at the same time, in a creepy kind of way, it was nice to see the perfectionist see that she wasn't so perfect. She always seemed to point out my flaws, so now I got to see that someone else noticed that she had a few of her own.

My grandmother said, "Well you have to remember that you also have a family. You can't be at work this late.

Your husband tried to call you and couldn't reach you. Did you call here? Did you forget that we were coming today? I thought we talked about going to dinner on the phone." My grandmother offered a barrage of questions that you already knew that she had the answers to, but asked it anyway to let you know that you didn't do what you were supposed to do.

My mother sidestepped all those questions and said, "No, I didn't forget, and it's still early enough, so let's go." She gave my grandmother an unapologetic look, though. My mother loved work and it didn't matter what you said or did. She was going to work as much as she could. I actually think that when my mother eventually retired and stopped working it did her more harm than good.

We didn't get home from dinner that night until after 10 p.m. but it was the weekend so it was ok. We all came home and fell out in our beds, tired from the week and enjoying our food comas until the next morning. For many years, almost 40, my mother worked tirelessly. *My mother's first love is work.* There was no balance many times between her job and her homelife. I wonder if it laid the foundation for what she is struggling with today. No exercise, not enough water, lots of coffee, soda pop, hardly any lunch at times, or sleep. It makes me wonder if it all could have been handled differently. I wished for her sake, and our sake, that it had.

Chapter Three

❧❦❧

She Won't Even Catch a Cold

always admired the way that my mother was tough. I was reared in Michigan and my mother was born and reared in Columbus, Ohio. She grew up in tough winters in Ohio, just as I did in Michigan. BUT....I can't stand winter time because of the dreary and cloudy skies, the dark nights that begin at 4:00pm and the stinging cold that comes with it.

My mother could spend her whole adult life in schools surrounded by germy, "walking-petri dishes" also known as beautiful children--and never get sick. I, on the other hand, would start sneezing and sniffling if I stood too close to the front door during the first Michigan snowfall. I could feel the chill in my bones through the door and my feet felt like ice for hours, even with thick socks and warm bedroom shoes. It didn't matter, I figured out early on that after dealing for years with thunder snow, cold rains, cloudy days, ice storms, snow storms and snow that fell sideways that pelted your face....I could not remain in such weather and have my sinuses survive. I would catch all kinds of colds, sinus infections, ear infections. And let's not forget the childhood torture and horror of the dreaded chickenpox that ravaged my house in the 80s. My mother would bathe me and my two brothers head to toe every morning before going to work. She would manage to side step the same chickenpox that would take down and hospitalize some adults. I cannot gather enough words to thank the makers of the chickenpox vaccine to this day to eradicate such a terrible virus among children.

Because of this, I saw my mother for so many years as not only brilliant, but so tough and so strong. Nothing could take her down. Nothing could take down her spirit, so how in the world did she "catch" dementia, when *she won't even catch a cold?*

In summer of 2008, I decided to take my children, who were very young then, up to Michigan to visit and see what I could do to help my mother. She spent all of her retired years thus far taking care of my very elderly grandmother who had Alzheimer's. My mother was strong, but during these years, I wish she would have allowed others to help her when they offered. No one is that strong for that many years. No one.

Michigan has some of the longest and most beautiful summer days in June. The sun won't set until around 9:45 p.m. The sky will look like it's 7:00 pm when it's almost 10:00 at night. There is nothing like it in the world.

My elderly grandmother was trying to get ready for bed.

My children were already bathed and in the bed, so I went into my grandmother's room to help. My mother says wearily,

"Go on, I got it."

"Well, okay," I responded, "But I came here to help. Why don't you just let me help? I can get her pajamas on. Then this will give you some time to take care of yourself and get yours on, too. I know you are tired."

She thinks about it and responds, "Alright," and walks quietly into her room.

I turn and smile at my grandmother who wanted her hair to be rolled up and she handed me the first roller. I took the roller and gently turned some hair around the barrel of the roller before attaching the clamp. My grandmother's silver and silkened hair made me smile. I remember when she used to religiously dye her hair to keep the grays away, and now it was a silver crown of glory.

After rolling her hair, and putting her into her pajamas, I told Mother that I was going to check on my mom to see if she was ok but I hadn't heard any movement in her room since she left.

I found my mom on the side of her bed with a small bottled water and a pair of deep blue colored pills. Medicine? My mother never takes medicine. She is just like her father, my grandfather, who never got sick. Since I hate swallowing pills, and my mother never takes medicine for anything, I especially paid attention to what she was doing.

"What is that?" I curiously asked pointing to the pills.

"Oh, it's nothing," she said and briskly swallowed the pills before I could get an answer. This "nothing" meant in her language: I don't wanna talk about it.

"Mom, you never get sick, so what medicine is this? Are you ok?" I asked with concern.

"Oh yes, I'm fine," she said wearily. She was so tired. I could hear the exhaustion in her voice. Then she showed me the medicine in the packet for sleeping pills. I could feel the muscles in my face begin to tense up. For me, any type of medication for my mother is very strange, indeed.

"Why do you need sleeping pills? How long have you been taking these? You can't sleep through the night anymore?"

"Well, sometimes Mother gets up in the night to go to the bathroom, or your brother comes in here and has been drinking, and then my sleep gets messed up."

"Whaatt??" I exclaimed. Then I started to get a little annoyed. *So why is he still here??*

"Ok Mom, this is your house and you already know that. So, put him out! Why does he live here for free anyway? You don't have to put up with him doing that. If Mother needs help going to the bathroom, have you thought about a geriatric potty for her so that she won't have to travel across the hall? Maybe she will have less chances of falling, too."

I desperately wanted to be the "problem solver" for my mother.

"It's not that important…" she begins to brush me off.

I retorted angrily, "Oh yes it is! Are you going to listen to me? I have never seen you do this before. I don't think it's healthy. Why can't you take melatonin instead? It's a natural sleep aid for the body. You need help, Mom. Why don't you just hire someone to come in and help you with the housework and laundry or something. What about your sisters? They have tried to help before…"

She cuts me off and says very curtly, "It's fine!"

Suddenly my grandmother yells from her room, "Ok! I'm fixin' to say my prayers, now."

That's usually the cue that she is ready to take her medicine. As I walked out of the room to my grandmother, I thought to myself, *please say some prayers for my mom, too…*

I helped my grandmother take her pills and swallow her water. Then helped her turn around where she wanted to kneel in prayer on the floor. After a few minutes, she signaled to be helped into bed. I tucked her in under the covers and gave her a kiss on her forehead, and said, "Goodnight,

Mother." She smiled lovingly and closed her eyes to go to sleep.

After turning off her light and closing up her door, I was hoping to continue the conversation with my mom. But when I returned, she had already gone off to sleep. I turned off her TV and her lamp on her crowded nightstand and let her rest.

The next morning, I decided I would get up and make breakfast for everyone in the house. There was orange juice, strawberry yogurt, croissants, jam, fresh fruit, cereal, and some turkey sausage. I looked at my menu and felt happy that I could do something to lighten my mother's responsibilities while I was there, but I made a mental note that I indeed was going to do something to bring in some outside help. No more sleeping pills.

My kids woke up and as their noses would have it, came immediately downstairs in their pajamas to fill up those stomachs that I call bottomless pits! Then my youngest brother Marcus came to visit the kids and play baseball with them in the backyard. My mother came downstairs, entered the kitchen, and stared at the food for a moment. Then she said,

"I'm going to make some scrambled eggs with cheese, hashbrowns and more sausage."

"Oh, ok, well that's going to take longer. I thought we

would go downtown to the waterfront and let the kids play in the sprinklers on the river. I can make it all if you want. I see that you still have to get dressed."

"No, I'll do it," she confirmed with a no-nonsense tone and she began to pull out extra food and pans.

"Are you sure? We can always grab lunch on the water. The kids love that, so that's why I made a light breakfast," I reminded her.

"No. It's ok, I got it," she said without even looking at me. She went about noisily getting pots and pans and prepared to add to what was already done. The problem was, it took away from the day's scheduled plans. Almost an hour later, my mother was loading up the eggs, hash browns, extra turkey sausage and orange juice on my grandmother's plate, including the fresh fruit, yogurt and croissants that were prepared earlier. That was a lot of food to eat at one sitting. She then put it on a breakfast tray and tried to proceed up the steps on her brand new thick, carpeted floors in her long robe and bedroom shoes.

At that point, my brother Marcus came in from the back yard with a couple of my kids and said, "Hi Mom. What are you doing? I thought breakfast was already made? Did you eat yet?" And he gave her a hug. When he looked down and saw her carrying the tray, he asked "Is all that food for Mother?"

"Yes," she responded over her shoulder as she turned to

climb the stairs with the tray of food.

"Well, here, let me carry it for you. If we are going downtown, we need to get a move on. Then you can shower and everything while I take the tray up." It was already 1:00 p.m.

"No, I got it" as she had already started on her third stair. Marcus shook his head in disbelief and didn't say any more because he already knew it was useless to keep making suggestions. I said nothing and while looking at him, shrugged my shoulders.

He whispered to me, "Was there something wrong with the breakfast that you fixed?"

I whispered back, "I don't know. I hope not but she never said anything either way. I was trying to help."

Marcus nodded his head in a yes motion and said, "I know…"

We watched her go up the first landing of stairs. I started to go back into the kitchen to do dishes and clean up. Marcus started to go back to the backyard, when we both heard a very loud thud from upstairs. We both looked at each other at the same time and ran up the stairs together.

Our mother had somehow tripped and dropped the entire tray of food and drink all over the new carpet and partly on herself. I asked if she was alright and she said, "Yes, but

I dropped everything all over my new carpet!"

"Don't worry about the carpet" I said as I tried to help her up gently. Marcus picked up everything that had spilled from the tray and asked, "Now, will you let someone help you, Mom---please?"

Mom silently rolled her eyes, let out a sigh and went to the bathroom to shower and get dressed. In that language, that meant, "I know, you're right." But she won't admit it.

Meanwhile, my grandmother was still sleeping and hadn't heard a thing.

Fast forward to later that evening, we eventually returned from the water park with the kiddos. I sat down with my mother and asked her about what happened earlier that morning.

"Hey Mom,"

"Hey..." as she was just finishing watching one of her favorite TV shows, "Jeopardy."

"Was the breakfast that I made not enough for Mother?" I asked with all humility.

"What?" she asked.

"You know, the breakfast from earlier. What happened? I hated to see you fall like that after all of that work."

"I don't know..." she said.

"Would you consider bringing in someone to help you with cooking, laundry and other stuff to help take some of the weight off, Mom? I am getting concerned about your health. You can't go down taking care of Mother all by yourself."

"I can't trust anyone here. I don't want anyone in my house."

"But Mom, they have certified companies that have certified nurses and people who are licensed, bonded and insured. They have to pass background checks and everything."

"No, it's ok. I like my house and I am not going to have any strangers in my house."

"Ok, well what about an assisted living? They have places especially made for those dealing with dementia or Alzheimer's these days? Mother is sedentary all day sitting which is not healthy. She needs to have those that are trained to help keep her moving. She is having more accidents, Mom. We have to do something and this could be a great help for you and Mother. It's not like back in the day," I suggested.

"No! I will not put my mother into a nursing home," she assertively replied.

"That's not what I said, Mom. But please listen and hear me out…"

"No!" she replies stubbornly.

I held my breath and presented the brochures anyway for her to look at when she had come to a calming point. "Mom, I picked up these brochures while I was out today at a couple of places. Just try to read them. While I am here, maybe we can go and take a tour together."

"No. I don't want anyone to mistreat my mother," she quips.

"I agree. I don't either. And she is my grandmother and I love her. But you are my mother! Don't make a sweeping generalization like this about every place. The money is there to cover the services whether it's inbound or at a place. I just want you to stay around longer, be healthy and enjoy your own children and grandchildren---*just like she did when she was your age, Mom.*"

Mom doesn't respond. She instead picks up her crossword puzzle book and goes back to her puzzle that she wasn't even working on when I walked in earlier because she was looking at Jeopardy. In her language, that means, "Leave me alone. I know you are probably right, but you won't get it out of me today, lady!" I took my cue and stopped talking, but kept praying.

Well, my mother never did agree to the help.

So let's talk about bad timing. Later that night, it's around 3 a.m. and I am sound asleep. I feel someone shaking my shoulder. When I opened my eyes, I saw my mother in her pajamas, but she had on a jacket and her purse was on her shoulder. I heard the jingling of keys in her hand as she jostled them around. I immediately sat up! I thought something had happened to my grandmother and she was trying to get her to the hospital. But no....she whispers,

"Lenny called and he has run out of gas..."

"What?" I questioned in disbelief. "Where is he? Does he have money for a cab to catch a ride here?"

"No, so I am going to get him..."

"Hold on! Mom, no! Are you kidding me? Are you asking for a deathwish?"

"Look," she starts towards the door, "I am going to pick him up and come right back.

"Where is he, Mom? Let me go and get him then and you stay here with Mother and the kids. Everyone is asleep." I jumped out of bed and grabbed clothes and a jacket to put on with my driver's license and car keys.

"No, he's been drinking, so I will go."

"Mom this is ridiculous. Why don't you call the police to have them come and pick him up? It will serve him right."

"Ok, I am leaving," and she goes downstairs.

This was a terrifying decision because I didn't want to leave my kids or my elderly grandmother sleeping alone in the house with no protection, but then again if my brother had been drinking, who knows how he would treat her? So, I knew I had to go.

I asked again, "Mom, where is he?"

"He is only about a mile away. I am leaving the car there until morning when he can go back and put gas in it tomorrow."

We found him sitting in a quiet and clean neighborhood. No foot traffic. He seemed so out of place in that neighborhood waiting in that car. When we pulled up, he was sitting in his car. He looked as if he was sleepy. We didn't have to blow the horn because he heard my mother's car. He turned his face to see me sitting there, and the look of disdain crossed his brow. *Good,* I thought, *because I am about to get deep in it tonight if he says the wrong thing to me or my mother!* ...And of course...he did. He began yelling and talking to my mother and asking why I had to come with her to pick him up?

He never said sorry. He never said thank you. He just talked to my mother like he was a street pimp complaining about what she did. *Oh, helllllllll no!* At that moment, I figured I would holler now and rebuke and forgive much later. He pressed the "Mama" button, and that was it!

I desperately wanted to choke him, but somehow I was restrained from touching him so I let it rip with my mouth! Sorry, God, but I knew nothing about being humble, sweet, or kind that night and I said a lot of things to my brother that let him know that I would basically have no problem drop-kicking his behind in the middle of the street for putting my mother and me through such foolishness. It was very ugly and it was to the point that we were all yelling in the car at each other. We almost had an accident over him!

Immediately, I called my dad to tell him what happened. It's in the middle of the night and I knew he would be in deep sleep by now, but since he lived literally 5 minutes away from my mother, I called him instead of the police. As I dialed his number from my cell phone, I let the phone ring and ring until I heard his sleepy greeting over the phone. I apologized profusely for waking him, but I was in the middle of wanting to hurt my brother or throw him in jail. I knew that neither of my parents wanted me to do that, so that's why I called my dad. While all of this is happening, my brother is cursing and yelling in the backseat and laughing. When we pulled up to my dad's place, and he saw him standing there getting himself dressed with his coat, he quieted down. My dad is a gentle giant, but he didn't play with my brother. There are many factors as to why my brother turned out differently than Marcus and me, but my dad did what he was supposed to do as a father. However, the power of an enablement can destroy what was invested and cause others to shrug their shoulders and eventually turn away to save themselves.

The next morning I called Marcus and told him what happened. He was livid! My brother Marcus is an athlete and is about 6'1 tall and muscular. He was mad! He came straight over to the house and knocked on my mother's door. He proceeded to go down to the basement and haul Lenny upstairs to the den. I made all of my kids go upstairs to watch TV in my Mom's room and shut the door.

"Lenny, please let me know what suit and tie you like the best and what colors will match nicely against your skin."

Lenny wrinkled his brow and looked confused. As Marcus guarded the door inside the room where both Lenny and my mother were gathered, I proceeded to recall the foolishness of the few hours before. I concluded with this statement:

"That's not only your mother, but she is our mother, too. You don't have the right to put her in danger or stress her out. Do you know why I asked you what you wanted to wear?"

He quietly shook his head no.

And in the quietest crazy whisper I made it fiercely and angrily known:

"Mom, if Lenny ever does this again, you call the police and call for a squad car to pick him up. You are not to put yourself in harm's way for him. He knew when he left home that he didn't have any gas. He is 32 years old. He is not a baby! Lenny, I asked you what you wanted to wear because that's what I will *bury* you in if you **EVER** in your life put the life of our mother or my children's, or mine, or our grand-mother's lives in danger again by coming out in the middle of the night to come and pick you up. You **KNEW** she was going to sacrifice her safety and well being to get you. Don't you **EVER** do that again. Because if I **EVER** get a phone call that something has happened to my mother because of you, I **WILL** take you out!" I didn't mince my words and **I meant every word I said**. My blood was boiling because I had become hot. I broke into a sweat in the middle of an air conditioned room. I had had enough! Luckily for his sake, he never put my mother through an episode like that ever again. Marcus nodded in agreement with me and I signaled that it was ok to unblock the door. Lenny knew that we were serious.

My grandmother and my brother who lived in the base-ment both got progressively worse over the next few years. The stress was taking more of a toll on my mother. I tried to call for help from her siblings and they responded, but my mother still decided to not accept help, nor let go of my grandmother.

So...frustrating....but moving forward....

Chapter Four

———— ❦ ————

Pass the Baton

n January 2014, my beautiful grandmother passed at the age of 92. She and my grandfather led a life-well lived and legacies to follow. My grandmother started to show signs of dementia in her 80s, so I "get it." But still, having this disease is not a normal part of aging.

My mother never enjoyed one day of her retirement since she retired in 2006. She dedicated herself to the full time care of my grandmother. I am all for it because I can't stand the poorly run nursing homes, either. I grew up visiting lots of older relatives in nursing homes that smelled like urine, were understaffed and patients went through constant theft of their belongings and valuables. Not all nursing homes are this way, but the ones I visited were. There have been many improvements to many nursing/rehabilitation/assisted living places since the 1980s.

Here's what I didn't know when I tried to talk to my mother about getting outside help: In order to put your relative into the nursing home, they must turn over their homes, or any other valuable assets over to this system. This is even for those who may have retirements. I know there are many that are priced differently, but this is America, right? You get what you pay for.

Pause.

How does a person work all of his or her life and then have to give everything over and leave nothing for your children or other family members?

Why do we work and retire with "benefits" if we still have to give up everything in the very end when the care is much more needed? Am I missing something? It's too much. In order for my grandmother to go into a nursing home, the family home in Ohio and anything else would have to be turned over. Then there are the legal wranglings and paperwork that come from turning over every valuable you have to get the care. I know that proper, skilled care is not free, but how is it that nursing home attendants and aids are so underpaid when the system they work for is taking over people's property and valuables?

So, my mother never learned that she needed to accept help when others were desperately trying to help her.

I was sitting on my deck in the summer of 2014 enjoying quiet time when one of my sons came outside with my cellphone. Apparently there had been at least 4 missed calls from some of my aunts and uncles.

"Mom here's your phone. It keeps ringing off the hook," says William, my oldest.

"Thanks, dear," I said as I took the phone and scanned the calls. I became a little nervous. I know that earlier during that year, Mom agreed that she would choose me to be her Power of Attorney over her health care and finances should something ever happen to her. It was a good conversation, but I didn't move on it then, and I don't really know why. But when I kept getting all of those calls, I got concerned. Maybe something had happened to my mother and they were trying to reach me in an emergency?? With my fingers shaking I pressed the key to return the call to one of my uncles.

"Hello?" He asked.

"Hey Uncle, how are you? Everything ok?"

"Oh yes, everything is fine, I just needed to ask how your mom was doing. I know things are different for her now that Mother is gone," he said.

"Yes, taking care of Mother was a full time job for many years for her. I keep getting all of these calls from everyone today. Have you heard anything? I am going to call Mom after I talk to you."

"Calls from who? I was just checking in on you and your mom, that's all. I do think that we need to do something about getting your mom examined to make sure that she is ok."

"That should have been done a long time ago. My mother's doctor was supposed to do all of this and look in on Mother, too, and she never did it. There's only so much that I can do living so far away."

"Do you think she would move?" He asked the silent question hanging in my head.

"Hard to say, but my guess is no. She loves her house and her space. She probably wouldn't, but I will see…" I answered and then let my voice trail off.

We both said our eventual goodbyes and hung up. Before I called my mother, I checked the voicemails on my cell phone. They were from most of her siblings who were concerned about my Mom. Then I called my mother, and she sounded fine. I saw that I missed a call from Marcus, my baby brother, so I called him back.

"Hi Marcus did you call me earlier?"

"Yep, look, I don't know about Mom staying by herself with Lenny anymore."

"I know but she doesn't want to put him out and she doesn't want to leave her house. I can't force her, Marcus."

"Oh yeah? Wait til you hear this. I am sitting here visiting with Mom last Saturday and watching TV. You know when someone calls the house, their name and phone number is put on the TV screen. So I saw it was Tylea's name and number. I didn't think anything of it, but then I heard Mom talking to her like she was a stranger."

"What? What do you mean a stranger?" I asked

"Well, I started listening to what she was saying and do you know that chicken head was trying to scam money out of Mom? And she thought she was going to get away with it!"

"What?!" I exclaimed.

"Yeah," he continued, "She didn't know Mom was not alone and that her cable company projected a person's full name and phone number on the TV screen. She tried to act like she was somebody from the UNCF asking for money for the college fund."

"Oh my God!" I was fuming, "What happened next? I remember now, Tylea is one of Lenny's girlfriends."

Marcus continued, "I took the phone from Mom. I told her I was going to report her to the police and the UNCF. She is crazy and evil for trying to do that! We gotta get Mom away from Lenny."

I silently agreed, but how? I also was in shock because I had just talked to my mother and she said *nothing* about this problem with Tylea. My mother and Lenny were in a toxic mother and son relationship and the only way that it would end is through death, or having one of them physically removed. I am convinced that they can't even live in the same state. I knew that I had to make some hard decisions and have some truthful conversations about all of this. If I waited on Mom, it would never happen. My parents had divorced years ago, and though they remained friends, my dad could only go so far with looking out for her. I saw that no one else was doing it. I decided that this would be the summer to go home and take mom to be examined by doctors, get the paperwork going for the power of attorney status and make the necessary police reports. This has got to stop and for some reason, *the baton is being passed to me.* So I grabbed it and began my race by pouring my heart out to God:

Oh my God, give me strength! I never knew my family would end up like this. But why me? Why is this being handed to me? Why my family? Didn't my mother sacrifice enough and do the honorable thing? And is this what we get? This is horrible. Why didn't she get any rest and take care of herself. Why didn't she fight for balance in her life? My mother seemed to melt her whole well-being physically, mentally, emotionally into my grandmother. But what about us? What about your own children and grandchildren?

My ranting and raving of questions and thoughts in my prayer just carried on and on in my head until I forced myself to go for a walk. She has sacrificed too much of herself. Just because you become a caregiver does not mean that you are to become a martyr. There is only one person who sacrificed Himself for the world and He is now seated at the right hand of the Father in heaven. After Him, there is no more. Did she forget that the job was already taken? Too many questions and not enough answers.

Chapter Five

She Already Has a Name

n July of 2014, I drove 500 miles with my then boyfriend, Jeremiah, to take my mother to the doctor. I
usually love coming home! It is where I grew up and
where I gain strength to go back out into the crazy and
unforgiving world. But this time it was different, I was
forced to take on the heaviness of taking on the role of
caregiver for my mother. It was heavy because my mother
was so much younger than my grandmother when she was
diagnosed with dementia. My grandmother was well into
her 80s; however, my mother was diagnosed at the age of
68. She may have had it earlier than that age, but this was
the age of the official diagnosis. And all of my life, my
mother has been the strong and capable one. I couldn't
imagine seeing her any other way. Mom didn't want to go
to any of these appointments and it was tough convincing
her to go. In my prayers, I had to ask God to strengthen
me because this was definitely unchartered territory for
me. I was battling against her resistance and feeling like
the "parent."

"Mom, we are coming up to take you to the doctor and see what's happening with you."

"Nothing is wrong with me. I am fine."

"When's the last time you been to the doctor?"

"I don't know! Why do we have to do this again? Who said I needed you to take care of me anyway?"

"Well, Mom, you have been tired for a long time in dealing with Mother and now we have to take care of you. You said that you felt comfortable with me being your power of attorney, remember? Do you know that all of your siblings have called me in the last 2 weeks to ask about you and your welfare?"

"*What?*"

Sigh. "Well, Mom, it's my turn now and I would be honored if you allowed me to do so for you."

My mother sighs in response while I silently and awkwardly wait on the other end.

"Well, you are always welcome to come home. You know that. Alright. I will see you when you get here. You both be safe and tell Jeremiah hello. Love you, babe."

"Love you, too Mom. See you soon!" Whew! This was too much for me. I don't like "parenting" my mother. It was like someone had flipped the script.

Fast forward. Mom was tested with blood work, blood pressure readings, an interview with the neurologist and nurse, and an hour long of cognitive testing by both her internist and the neurologist. For this portion of the testing, I waited out in the waiting room. During this process, I could tell that she was a little nervous and uncertain. At every step of the way, I reassured her that it was not going to hurt and not going to cause her any pain. I also took her to get an MRI for her brain. At the same time, I went ahead and secured an attorney who was a friend from high school to do the power of attorney paperwork who was reasonably priced. I thought about the expense of this process; it is expensive. I thought about those who are in need of such paperwork and what happens if they don't have the money to secure it. By the time you find the lawyer and pay the retaining fees it can cost quite a bit. Unless you know how to do the research and know how to secure some of these services through agencies that are dedicated to the elderly and seniors, you really won't know. They are not marketed or discussed on commercials, billboards, in any church I have ever attended or visited. We don't talk about this enough in our society until it happens to someone we love. *Why?*

Unfortunately, my own mother was diagnosed with dementia at stage 1 having mild cognitive memory loss with the neurological brain changes that will lead eventually to

Alzheimer's disease. She was only 68 at the time of her diagnosis. I know that dementia can happen at even earlier ages than this, but how and why? The diagnosis was read and written to me in an email detailed from the neurologist. My mother was deficient in Vitamin D and her blood pressure was getting high. The neurologist prescribed the medication that she needed. We also came together to have a family meeting with my dad and my brothers to talk about the diagnosis and what it meant in terms of diet and lifestyle changes. We didn't like having this happen, but we learned that it was a combination of diet, white processed sugar, the stress of living a caregiver's life, and the stress of living with Lenny and his issues—family dynamics and relationships in a stressful environment. After talking her through her diagnosis and what it meant, I asked her to come with us down South and not remain in that house. My grandmother was at peace resting, and my brother could figure out his life. Marcus was in agreement and then, so was Mom.

My brother Marcus and I are about 8 years apart, but he had an old soul like me, and we could get along better as kids growing up, than with Lenny. Lenny was always spirited. He was the first boy born into our family, but the middle child just like my mother. From the ages of 4 to 8, Lenny was my best friend. Then, he changed. My mother always wanted the boy to be born first, and then the girl. It should not have mattered, but it did to her. It came out in the differences of how we were all treated in our childhood. Lenny knew this and took advantage of it. But for years, Lenny was allowed to get away with behaviors like name-calling, bad grades, hitting, taking things out of my room, not respecting my privacy in the bathroom or my bedroom, getting my bike stolen, and never facing any consequences. I could NEVER get away with these kinds of behaviors. Hands down--Lenny was enabled. My father did what he needed to do, but a lot of times his authority was usurped behind his back from my mother. Ladies and gentlemen, this is how you create trouble in your marriage and in your child. It only gets worse. He then felt entitled, arrogant and now we have a drinking habit. The combination is toxic and deadly. When he didn't drink, he was my brother and a nice person. But when he drinks, he is a mean drunk. It is dangerous to become so enthralled with something that you are not in control of what you say or do. He is never sorry for what he says or does. I wish that our relationship was better. I miss my brother and I want him back. Whenever I go home, I always loved sharing the bed with my mom. As we were going to bed later that night, the last thing I remembered after putting the kids to bed was my mother staying up late to work on her crossword puzzles. When I awakened again, I had a creepy feeling. I felt someone standing over me, but I thought I was dreaming. I opened one eye at the clock on the nightstand and it said, 2:37 a.m. We were leaving early that morning in a matter of hours. When I continued to turn over, I saw a shadow and it was the silhouette of Lenny standing over me while I slept! I didn't know whether to hit him or yell at the top of my lungs. Before I could say anything, he stood there with his hands in his pockets and calmly said,

"I know you think you are going to do something by being here, but you're not..."

"Lenny are you crazy? What do you want? You don't stand over anyone while they are sleeping. Have you lost your mind! Go to bed!"

"Did you hear me?" He asked.

"I know you better hear me and take your behind to bed and leave me alone. You'll wake Mom."

"So! In the end, I'm going to win, not you, just wanted to let you know that."

"You are a liar where you stand! Congratulations! Let me know when you make it to the final round. Now leave me alone, or Mom is going to wake up if I have to jump out of this bed!

He chuckled and walked back downstairs into his dungeon of a basement. The thought of violence does enter my mind here...but I digress...let's continue...

I drove my mother in her car, and some of her belongings with us back to Tennessee to get away from the growing dysfunctional spirit in her household. Jeremiah drove the car that we drove in originally and followed us back South. She allowed Lenny to drive her car, and not return it with any gas in it, and sometimes with scratches in the paint that weren't there before he drove it. It was one of Lenny's girlfriend that was compromising her credit card and other finances. *But she wouldn't put him out of her house??? Why did she allow this?* All I could do was shake my head and try to help her, if she wanted the help. Everyone enjoyed her staying with us and we were hoping that she would stay. Jeremiah would come and visit after seeing about his own mother across town. But each day, if Lenny called my mother, he was whispering in her ear about money, money, money. It was as if he was going through a withdrawal.

The kids loved having her around. I loved having her around. We took her to lunch on her birthday. We went to the movies, did shopping--if it was fun--we did it for her. One day I wanted to take her for a pedicure and here's how this conversation went:

"Hey Mom, I am going to get a pedicure. You want to get one with me?"

"No."

"Have you ever had a pedicure before? It's like getting a foot bath and getting a nice massage. It's a nice treat for yourself."

"No that's alright. I don't want anybody touching all over me." She turned back to her crossword puzzles.

I sighed and chuckled. "Ok, no worries, I'll be back when I am done."

Dementia or not, I still needed my mother, too. You never get too old or too far gone in life that you don't love and miss your parents. I decided that *she already has a name* and it's definitely not dementia. And I am not going to let you take her. My mother's identity would not be usurped by a disease or even the mentioning of its name. I am not going to let this disease take over her life, or define who she is. I decided to help her fight because I would want someone to help me fight, too. But I forgot one important thing, she didn't help me to help her, too.

Chapter Six

———— ❧❧ ————

So She Left

So she left. After my mother was first diagnosed in 2014, we brought her with us down South. School was now back in session and the kids were back in school. I was back teaching in the classroom. Two weeks before, my mother joyfully agreed to come to my classroom and help me get some things set up for my students. I saw how she felt so at ease in the school building and I asked if she wanted to become a volunteer with my school. She smiled and said yes without any hesitation. I was happy too. The doctor said to keep her socializing and doing things to keep her busy and moving. Since my mother loved to work anyway, this would be a welcome change for her in the house.

After working in the classroom on the last day before school started, I had to stop at the store to get some last minute minor school supplies for my students. We walked by a big sign that boasted of sale prices on pop for the hot summer weekend that was quickly approaching. It was my least favorite drink--dark sodas. Those cans of poisons are not good for anyone, yet they are pushed out into our country like they are golden. The neurologist also warned to keep her away from any type of sodas, especially the dark and artificially flavored or colored pop that would exacerbate the brain changes for her disease. Sugar, in any of its processed forms, like white sugar is terrible for the human body. Over time, it forms plaques in the brain that affect the amygdala (pronounced ah-MIG-dah-la). This area in the brain holds our memories as well as the other areas of the brain such as the prefrontal cortex that deal with short-term memory loss.

Mom exclaims, "Ooooh! I want to get these. They are on sale!"

"I don't think that's a good idea Mom. You have been drinking sodas, but we have to find some other healthier choices to drink. Not to mention that you already had been drinking sodas since you came down from Michigan."

Her eyes rolled and she began to become resistant.

"No I haven't. This is a good sale and I shouldn't pass it up."

"I like a good sale too Mom, but is it at the expense of your health?"

"Well, I am getting them."

"When are you going to start caring about yourself? You have worn yourself down completely for Mother. You wouldn't accept help for years. You refused to listen. And even now that I have come up there to help you and get you away from Lenny and the craziness, and after a diagnosis which I believe really shouldn't have happened at all, you would continue to willingly pump this poison into your body--because it's on sale?" Ummmm.....did someone say upchuck?

I snatched the cart and started walking towards the school supplies section because I had just gotten angry with my mother and in public. I don't care how old I get, I was raised old school and that was never back talking or getting attitude with your mother...period! I knew I was in smacking range so I needed to move quickly!

But surprisingly, she followed behind me looking shocked and still mad because she couldn't have her sodas. I got the supplies and paid for them. I decided that we needed to go to dinner and talk this out.

We arrived at the Chinese food restaurant and I asked for a booth in the back corner. We were still operating in silence until I came with an apology.

"Mom, I'm sorry. But this has been hard for me to deal with more than I thought."

"Ok," she responded with an aloof tone.

"I am upset that this happened. Since Mother had it, I don't know if it could have been avoided, but I know this came on way too soon for you. I also think what if I get it too?"

For the first time since our spat, she looked at me with interest and wonder.

"No, you'll be fine," she calmly replied and stirred her hot tea.

"Mom, I hope so, but I need you to be fine. I need you to understand that I am only trying to help. I am not trying to parent you. But would you want me to keep doing things to hurt myself if I was already diagnosed with something that is not going to go away?"

She didn't respond.

"Mom, I can help you fight. I know this is hard, Mom. But you have to fight, too. I can't do this without you. And I'm truly sorry. If you want, we can go over the diagnosis again if you need more explanation," I offered. How do you deal with a diagnosis such as dementia? You have seen what it did to your own mother and now...you? My mom is sometimes hard to read. I do know that she lives in denial about somethings. I would hear her from time to time saying that she is getting older and forgetful. She gets frustrated and maybe even angry. I hate it for her.

"No, it's alright. I understand," she said with a weak smile and ate her food. We both ate in silence.

The next morning, we did our usual schedule of going to school and mom was up at her usual time and pace. This particular morning was unusual because she decided that she would walk me out to my car, which she never used to do. She was smiling and seemed in pleasant spirits. School ended usually at 2:30 so I told her when I got back maybe we could go shopping. I pulled out of the driveway and drove off to work.

When I returned later that afternoon, her car was gone. I felt like someone had come by and deflated my balloon. I parked my car and came in immediately into the house and called out her name. Jeremiah had not been by yet from his job, so I couldn't ask him. I got nervous because she didn't know her way around the city. I called her cell phone and no answer. I waited another 15 minutes and called again, and it goes straight to voicemail--you know like when people want to avoid your calls and push the button for it to go there and then make the excuse that "Oh my call must have dropped..." or something.

I called Jeremiah and asked if he had heard anything from her. She favored Jeremiah and loved to tell him things that she never would tell me. When he said that he hadn't heard from her, I knew she had probably gone back to Michigan. He suggested that I call my brothers and that he would come over right after his shift. I called Marcus and left a message because he is hard to catch on the phone. Then I called Lenny. He sends a text message that she is in Ohio and has stopped at the grocery store to buy what else?? Soda pop. Really??

She finally got home later that evening to Michigan around 8 or 9 pm. It took her 12 hours to drive home. Lenny sent me a text message that she had made it safely and had brought back a trunk full of pop for drinking. Ok, Lenny, well I guess you were right. You did get her back after all.

Oh Lord...here comes the next upchuck, sorry, just brace for it:

Fine! I am done. I had the nerve to tell God that I tried to help her. Tried to get her straight with her medicine. Tried to get her away from people who would take advantage of her and brought her to my home and this is what I get? Rejection...again? This took me back to my days of trying to gain her approval and acceptance for her to even tell me that she loved me. You would rather go back to the familiarity of dysfunction instead of find healing anew? Poor Father God...I didn't let Him get in a word edgewise....

Why am I the "clean up woman " anyway? I have to raise my own kids. I am working full time and about to start a doctoral program, so I don't need this crap. God, you handed me this torch, but I got burned. Why me? Why was it my job from over 500 miles away and she has people right there in the city? You don't want my help---then you don't want me...again....*so she left*. And for the next four years, I let her. So when it was my birthday, no phone calls, just text messages to wish me happy birthday. She never called me on her own and for the first few months when she got back to Michigan she wouldn't even take my phone calls. I called her anyway. She's my mother and I was going to continue to be her daughter and no anger in the world was going to change that bloodline or genetic DNA.

Chapter Seven

Denzel!

My mother has an undying and hopeless crush (forever) on the great movie thespian, Denzel Washington. I don't care what restaurant we are in, or if we are watching a commercial on television, my mother will find a Denzel look-alike and ask me if I agree that some random man looks like Denzel! Here are a couple of examples for you all to see how deep this really runs:

One summer in 2007, I had come up to vacation with Mom and brought my children with me. We are on our way to the grocery store to do some light food shopping and we are waiting for my mother to finally get in the car.

After about 17 minutes, she finally arrives and gets into the car. My daughter asks, "Gran, what took you so long?"

Without skipping a beat, my mother responds and says with a smile, "I had to get my hair and jewelry together in case I see Denzel at the grocery store….(as she giggles)…"

I respond by rolling my eyes and finally put the car in reverse to hurry up and get this woman to the grocery store!

If that doesn't convince you, here's another…

In 2016, my mother has come down for my oldest son's high school graduation and it's an exciting time. It is time for my mother to go to her hair appointment. She was not able to take care of her hair and keep it fresh. It was a beautiful soft and silver gray as she had inherited from my grandfather, but because of years of using home hair perms and burning her hair with curling irons every day, it had yellowed and was wilted. I finally had had enough of asking her to allow me to do her hair and her turning me down. I announced to her:

"Mom, come with me because I need to go and run an errand, ok? Do you want to come with me?" I asked.

My mother, who is always up for a road trip responded, "Sure!" She picks up her 75-pound purse (I am *not* kidding… that purse is at least 30 years old) and threw it on her shoulder on her 119 pound frame and proceeded to the door. She won't give up that purse. I have tried to buy her several purses, only to be rejected. I am kind of used to it. I know, I will just have my husband give her one and see if she will finally use it. She likes getting things from him.

I took her to go and see my hair stylist who I have trusted with my hair for the last 5 years. My mother has always worn a pixie cut for years since I could remember. So I made the arrangements to have her hair cut, shaped, conditioned and styled for her to look her best. During the process of styling, she motioned for me to come over to her. I got up from my seat to listen to her concerns.

"I don't know about this…" Mom's voice trails off.

"Why? What's the matter? I am right here watching and everything is going fine."

"But what about my hair?" she asks very slowly and carefully.

"What? Your hair is about to be sharp, miss lady!" I say with a smile.

She jokes, "Is it sharp enough for Denzel? I don't want to scare him away, now…" and she looks at me smiling. I sighed and shook my head in jest.

Really? Did you really just say this to me just now? I know she didn't…

I said jokingly, "Mom! Denzel don't live here. He is married. Give him a rest. You been chasing this man for years. Are you serious??" I try to say this with so much kindness, gentleness and respect, but man she won't let this man go. Poor Denzel, please give him his freedom.

"Well," she replies, "I can dream, can't I?" as she chuckles.

"Yes Mom. And who am I to take away your dreams. But let's give Denzel a vacation today, okay? I think he is tired today," I comically suggest.

My mother giggles as I return to my seat.

And lastly...for those of you who may not still believe...

In the summer of 2017, Jeremiah and I had just married and we had gone to Michigan for a short visit before I had to return South for my dissertation defense. I had gone to the grocery store early one morning and made sure to pick up her renewal prescription for her dementia medicine that is supposed to slow down the process of losing her memory. I had put some small groceries away and went to check on Jeremiah. Mom was in the den as Jeremiah was fixing her some hot tea and breakfast.

"Mom," I said cheerfully, "I picked up your renewed medicine." I noticed that there was a movie on, that was starring who? None other than Mr. Denzel Washington, himself. I knew that I was in for a battle. *Oh Lawd!*

"What medicine?" Mom asks.

"Your medicine to help your memory. Come on and take it with your water while I make your breakfast before you forget," I suggested this...right? I started towards the kitchen foolishly believing that she would have gotten up to follow me. *Nope!*

She yelled her response from the den: "I *AM* busy. I am watching Denzel! I'll remember to take it later." Ah, yes! The obvious brush-off.

Really? How you gonna remember? Isn't that the problem?

Nevertheless, I smiled and said, "Ok, no problem I will bring it to you instead."

She continues, "Nope, I ain't taking no medicine right now. I will take it later. Now you interrupting me and Denzel!" Mom snaps impatiently.

Lawd, help!

Chapter Eight

The Wealthy Unwealthy

t's January of 2017 and the phone rings. I am in the middle of writing one of the last chapters of my dissertation. I am also planning for my wedding that is scheduled to take place in the next three months. I look down at the phone. I am shocked to see that my mother's number is showing up on my cell number. She never calls me, so I am curious. I immediately pick up the phone,

"Hi Mom? You ok?"

She doesn't respond, instead I hear what sounds like a dragging sound on carpet. It is a familiar sound. Oh, yes, it is the sound of the door of the den in my mother's house.

"Mom?" I ask again.

"Yes, hold on, I was closing the door."

"Are you ok? Where are you?"

"I am fine. I am in the den, but I don't want your brother to hear me."

"Ok what's going on? Is he drunk and acting out of control again?"

"No." She cupped the phone receiver with her hand and said in a muffling whisper, "I don't have any money in my account."

Unheard of! My mother has a great retirement so I am a little confused.

"What?" I say in disbelief.

She says it again, "I don't have any money in my account. I went to check the balance today and it is in the negative. I am behind on my house insurance…."

"Whaatt?" My mother always handled the bills at the house and never missed. Even when she and my father were married. He made the bacon--they both did--but he entrusted her to handle the money as she saw best being the lady of the house.

"What happened?" I asked.

"I don't know," she admitted and I heard her sighing.

I knew that she was frustrated, so I offered, "What do you want me to do?"

"I don't know, maybe call the bank and see why I don't have any money right now."

"Mom, do you need any money right now from me? I can have Dad come over there and give you some money and I can pay him back later. I can also go to my bank tomorrow to deposit some into your account."

"No no no! I don't need any of that. I will get another check in a couple of days. I am fine. I am just trying to figure out why I can't save any money."

You already know what I was thinking, but I didn't say anything.

"Ok, well how about we get on a three-way call to find out what is going on with your bank. We can start a fraud investigation and see if they can pinpoint some transactions for you."

Long story short, Lenny had indeed done some fraudulent transactions, but the MOST of the fraudulent transactions were from my mother. Apparently, she had been going across the street to the ATM just about everyday taking out hundreds of dollars in cash and not remembering what or where she had put the money. There's no telling. I decided to help my mother open and close a whole new account with my power of attorney papers to get Lenny out of her account. But after I found out that Lenny had my mother get on the phone to cancel the fraud investigation, I was once again outdone and upset. My mother remembered nothing and only did what he told her to do. The operator at the bank recorded it as "a family matter" and no one even bothered to call me to let me know that the investigation had been closed. It was evident that the only way that her finances would be straight, is if they weren't living in the same house with each other. He has never had a steady job, nor paid any bills at the home. My mother has never bounced checks that I ever knew about, so this was a huge deal for her to call me and indirectly ask me for my help. I knew things were beginning to change.

Fast forward...

It is the following year and I have finished my dissertation and defense, gotten married to Jeremiah, and we are living life as newlyweds. It is the near end of a much deserved Spring break on a warm spring April day of 2018. My phone rings again and it's my mother.

"Hi Mom. How are you?"

"Good. There's someone who is going to be calling you in the next few minutes."

"What?" I had just muted the TV. "Who is it and what's it about?"

"Ok babe, thank you. Love you!" And she hangs up. Are we back to the hang ups again?

Not 30 seconds later, my cell rings with a strange number that I didn't recognize. Apparently because I was her power of attorney, this meant that she didn't tell me about an account that she had for retirement. Well, someone had been living off the account for at least the last 20 years and she was missing so much money that it made my head spin. By the time I had the conversation, I had moved from the chair to the floor and sitting there in disbelief. After speaking with the new financial security advisor, he told me what I needed to do in order to get on to the account with my mother. First of all, she never even told me she had this account! She was still using the account, too! Mom, how can I protect you, if you won't let me in? I bet Lenny knew of the account.

I am reminded of the time that I tried to ask my mother a few years back about having a will. Her parents, my grandparents who had less education and money than she, had wills.

"Mom, I know that you are ok with me being the power of attorney, but I need to know if you have a will?"

"Yes."

"Ok good. Where is it? Is it in the safe or someplace else?"

"I don't know. But I remember some years ago, I did have a will made. But now that your dad and I are divorced... things are different now..."

"Mom, you and Dad have been divorced for at least 14 years, you mean to tell me, you still have the original will?"

"I guess so."

"Mom, you must update your will, life insurance policies, bills, etc. that may have had Dad's name on it. What if something happens? God forbid. We, your children, need to know this."

She doesn't answer me, she just sits there listening to the TV play Jeopardy, her favorite show.

"I know this is hard and a little awkward Mom. But I have been through a divorce, too. Things are different for single mothers and we have to be right on top of business and more communicative because we carry it all on our shoulders, ok? I just know how things are about this and I want to make sure that you are not getting screwed. I will help you if you let me."

"Yes, I know."

"I would rather have my mother, believe me. But at the end of the day, business is business." I wondered if she knew all along where her will was and she just didn't want to tell me? Does Lenny know where it is? Probably, but in order to not risk an argument, I left it alone. In many of our households today, we are not talking about important paperwork, updating documents from life events, nor telling our family what to do in case of an emergency. Especially if you are single, or a single parent. Some may think, I don't have anything anyway. Wrong! Even if it's a pre-paid funeral and the expenses covered by a life insurance policy, get 'er done!

It's bad enough to have the loss of a family member, but when business is left hanging out in the wind, that's when wealth gets caught up into the tangles of Probate court which could costs thousands and thousands of dollars to resolve. Don't become a part of the *wealthy unwealthy*, where you have wealth accumulated and acquired but you don't do anything to secure it or let trusted people know what is happening in case life suddenly happens. Mind-boggling and mind-blowing decisions must be made.

Chapter Nine

Resistance is Futile

That following summer of June 2018, my husband, Jeremiah and I embarked on our usual nine-hour drive from the south to take my mother to her two annual doctor's appointments for her physical and her neurologist in Michigan. We had made it to my brother Marcus's house and had a restful night. We also made sure to stop by and take mom to dinner and spend some time with her. I made sure to let her know that we would be back to take her to the doctor the next day. She sighs and snaps, "Why? Why do I have to go to the doctor? I have already been and I am fine! I am not going to the doctor!" I didn't respond. I only nodded my head in agreement and ignored her response. *Why resist and try to reason?*

"Ok, Mom. Love you and see you soon!" I said with a weary smile.

"Ok babe, love you!" responded my mother cheerily---as if she never had an attitude about anything.

I woke early the next morning around 7:30 and gave my

mother her first wake up call. Here's how our conversation went:

Phone rings:

My mother answers, (sounds sleepy) "Hello?..."

"Goodmorning Mom. You ok?"

"Yeah, just sleeping," she answers sounding a little annoyed.

I continue in my cheery tone, "Do you remember that you have to go to the doctor today?"

"What?" Mom whines.

"Yes for the neurologist. I told you about it last night after dinner," I say calmly.

I hear my mother make this long and drawn out sigh as she answers with a flippant tone, "I don't need to go to the doctor! I have already been and I'm fine."

"Mom, come on...I have been taking you to the doctor every year since 2014. You have not been this year yet and it's time to go. I will be there to pick you up by 9:30. You have a 10am appointment." Now I am starting to feel like a nag.

Before she can say anything else to resist, I say in my most loving and cheery voice, "Okay Mom, I will see you soon. I will call you before I leave."

My mother rushed me off the phone and says, "Ok, bye," and quickly hangs up.

Well, dang...you are welcome!

My husband and I getting in the car to take my mom to her appointments. It is approximately 9 a.m. and we are getting the car warmed up so that we can head that way. As we are leaving my brother's driveway, I call her on blue-tooth speakerphone in the car. Of course, she recognizes my number...

My mom answers still sounding sleepy, "Hello?" *Is she still in the bed even though I called her at 7:30?* I thought.

"Hi Mom, we are on the way to pick you up."

"Pick me up for what?" she retorts.

"Mom...I called you this morning about your doctor's appointment, remember? We can't be late, and you are supposed to be ready!" I roll my eyes and start to ask God to give me some kind of patience from somewhere. Is she really getting this bad?

Mom says with pushback, "I don't need to go to the doctor!"

My husband hears the conversation and does a silent hand signal to end the call. I abruptly told my Mom good-bye and looked at him. He looks at me and gently says, "Let me give it a try, ok?" *Ok buddy, good luck!* I thought. I started snickering and thought, *Yeah, right. She won't even listen to her own daughter, why would she listen to you? My mother is stubborn.*

Jeremiah pulls out his phone, dials my mother's number and puts it on speaker as I continue to drive towards the house. My mother does have Jeremiah's number in her phone so she does recognize his out of state area code and number.

My mom answers cheerfully, "Well, hello there!" *Say what?*

Jeremiah smiles and coos, "Well hello doll, and how are you this morning?"

My mother gushes, "Oh doing fine! And yourself?"

Now wait a minute! She doesn't EVER answer the phone like this with me.

Jeremiah continues, "Oh wonderful. Look Mom, we are coming to the house in 10 minutes to take you to lunch and to the doctor and enjoy the day, ok?"

My mother had the nerve to say, "Oh really? Well let me get myself together so I can be ready!"

Really? Are you for real? Are you serious?

Jeremiah does a little more small talk and then says with a big grin, "Ok, doll, I will see you soon!"

Mom: "Okaaayyy!" as she giggles and hangs up the phone.

What tha….??

I am now driving with my mouth hanging open in disbelief. Did I not just call her three minutes before with the same information? She is talking to my husband like he is Billy Dee Williams or something! Really?? My husband looks at me with that cheshire cat grin on his face and says, "Guuurl, you better keep me around!" And starts laughing.

When we pulled into my mother's driveway, my stubborn and hard-headed mother was dressed and ready to go, standing *outside* her gate with her jacket and purse waiting with a smile. Unbelievable!

Jeremiah looks at me again and chuckles. He gets out of the car and walks over to greet my mother with a big hug. She is all smiles and hugs him back as if she hadn't seen him in five years even though it was just yesterday. He escorts her to the car by the elbow, opens up the car door and buckles her in with her seatbelt giving her the attention that she loves. No argument, muss or fuss...and she had the nerve to look at me and say with her sparkling smile: "Good morning how are you?" I just smile and nod and say, "Good morning, Mom. Glad to see you," I say in disbelief. She says, "Oh yes honey, it is good to be seen rather than viewed!" She and Jeremiah break into cackling laughs.

Ok, am I being punked right now? Let's get this car moving, please. What is the end result? Get her to the appointments. After I see and hear all of this, I know that *resistance is futile.*

Chapter Ten

I Am Sick and Tired!

had to make a heavy decision after that trip. My husband kept urging me to bring my mom back to the South. *No! We tried that before and what did she do?* So why open up that can of worms again? If she wants to be here with Lenny and have him drive her down into the tubes, then that's on her, not me. A lot of these decisions she could have made when she did have her memory intact. I now have a new husband, my children are entering into high school, college, the military. Life is going on at full speed in my house and I don't need any extra. I was tired from everything and everybody and I needed a break. Funny thing is, my mom needed a break because I found out after much discussion with her, that she has been tired for a very long time.

One beautiful summer morning, I noticed that the sun was brilliantly shining on the leaves in the trees, and the grass was looking more green and lush than usual, for some reason. I pondered many thoughts about bringing my mother with us back South. We had only two more days left on our trip. I earnestly and frankly prayed to God:

God, you know what happened before. Everyone says I should bring her home. What do you say? Maybe I should because I don't think she will last. She's not eating, the house is falling down around her. But I will not have her cause problems like she did before. I don't want to go against her Lord; she's my mother. I am struggling with the guilt of possibly walking away from her and my brother altogether. This is too much! Why me? Do you want me to do this?

Immediately the Holy Spirit responded in my spirit and asked me four words:

Would you regret it? And He said nothing else! He didn't have to because He answered all of the questions and statements that I prayed about with those four words.

I already knew the answer. Yes, I would. I would regret it if something happened to her and I could have done something to stop it before it was too late. I knew that I would not be operating in my own strength. I just had to be obedient. But it still didn't feel good. Does it ever? My motto has been to never live with regrets. When we live with regrets, we don't live authentic lives. That, all by itself is regrettable. He didn't even address my "woe is me" attitude and I now understand why. *Well, why not me?* There was something to learn about my mom, me, our relationship and the enabling and toxic relationship between she and my brother. I was certainly not up for another uncomfortable and difficult situation, but I took it on with the help and support of my husband. She came back, with the urging of her grandchildren, and has been with us since.

Okay! Break time. We are now about to venture back into our Sunday School and Vacation Bible School Days. Do you remember the story of Jacob and Esau in the Book of Genesis in the Bible?

I also asked God how to "see" my mother and her perspective more clearly. I had to do this because I wanted to overcome the feelings of rejection and anger that had burrowed deep in my heart, that I didn't know were there until these situations with her health appeared. I had to get over it!

My mother was overcome by being spiritually tired, or spiritually fatigued. Tired emotionally, physically, spiritually---just every area of your life is worn out. It makes me think of the phrase: "*I am sick and tired*" and then fill in the blank.

According to Genesis 25, Jacob and Esau were the fraternal twin sons of Isaac and Rebekah. The story discussed the favoritism the two parents showed to their selected twin, as well as the ever important loss of Esau's birthright due to Jacob's deception. A person's birthright means their rightful place and position of inheritance in the family. This was very important in the biblical days, as it is very important even today. When a person feels that they have been unjustly overlooked or ignored and is not given their rightful place of love, attention, that is needed in the family, due to human bias or favoritisms, etc. it does take a toll on that person and their family members negatively. There is nothing good about favoritism amongst children. It tears down relationships and builds deep seated resentment that sometimes doesn't come up until after the parents have died. It is destructive and can be passed down generationally. Enter--the spirit of fatigue or tiredness. Some may also call it weariness.

Regarding my mother, she was never given her rightful place. She was born the second of six children to God-fearing parents (my grandparents). However, they were scared to keep three girls and three boys on the straight path through the 50s-70s. They were exhausted trying to keep everything together with little money and only high school educations.

She was never the favored child and she felt neglected because of it. I heard her over many years talk about certain decisions or conversations that were held concerning her welfare that left her hurting and feeling ignored. Every time she got close to feeling loved or appreciated, here comes something or someone else "taking" something for people who didn't give her what was rightfully hers. What I have seen from the consistency of her conversations is that she was always being "knocked" out of her rightful spot or positioning of importance in the family; this set the course for dysfunction and directly had a negative impact on her perspective and reality when making decisions or choices. She was exhausted for having to fight her way and compete her way to success amongst her siblings to win her parents' approval. She may have already had it, but her perceptions did not tell her so. And thus, when my grandparents were getting older and sick, she stopped heaven and earth in her life to make herself the "martyr" so that she could finally have that approval and recognition that she so needed. She wanted to feel needed in order to feel validated and important because of these unresolved issues. Even if it meant at her own expense.

Therefore, she passed these unresolved issues to her own marriage and children--favoritism and all--which is how Lenny was enabled to live rent and utility free for over 20 years in her home. Yet, he was a part of the dysfunction that she needed in order to feel important. Vicious cycle. Lenny was enabled to be who he has become today.

Chapter Eleven

Forgiveness

*The LORD will perfect that which concerneth me: thy mercy, O
LORD, endureth for ever: forsake not the works of thine own hands
(Psalm 138:8).*

*Being confident of this very thing, that he which has begun a
good work in you will perform it until the day of Jesus Christ:
(Philippians 1:6).*

Just as my mother took care of my grandmother, I certainly knew that I was going to take care of my mother. She made sure to honor my grandmother and grandfather. I would do the same, whether we lived in a tent or a mansion. I was not going to have my mother in potentially unsafe conditions.

But I will say this, though I love my brother Marcus, I miss my brother Lenny. Don't forget, he was my first best friend on this earth. For some years, it was just Lenny and me. He was a nice little boy until the favoritism, unaccountability, hand-holding and coddling began. Any type of attention shown toward me or Marcus, was diverted to Lenny because of his misbehavior, crying fits or other shenanigans to get the attention back on himself. Then, he slowly turned into the creation who would in turn use alcohol as his drug to find his acceptance after making mistakes and disappointing my mother and deep down, himself. Another vicious cycle. But no one could break the two of them apart. No matter what. After some heavy soul-searching, I see why he has turned out the way that he has. Enabling and favoritism will not get any child anywhere in their lives. When you enable a child to live beneath their God-given potential, you are setting them up for epic failure and establishing the foundation of an addictive dependency between the enabler and the child.

I want peace.

This time around, it's about accepting peace in the situation and in ourselves. The way that I forgave my mother for her missteps with me, is the same way that I hope someday my own children will forgive me. No parent is perfect, even though my mom sure tried! It's ok to show your children that you make mistakes. And from what I learned from my amazing father is that you can apologize for your mistakes to your child and it doesn't take anything away from the parent's authority to do so. As a matter of fact, the child will actually take hold of accountability better when a parent admits their mistake and genuinely apologizes out of love and respect for the child and their relationship.

No one ever apologized to my mother or took accountability for "stealing her thunder" whether it was intentional
or not. Time is moving and marching on and we don't have
much time. Forgiveness is healing and good for the soul.
We can't heal in anger, or in pain. Sometimes there may not
come explanation. When we are blessed to have answers to
long-standing questions and seek to listen and understand
without judgment, that's when we move into the healing
epiphany of *forgiveness* and move forward on our journey.
I resisted this for some years, but I am now finally glad to
accept the honor and privilege of being my mother's keeper.
She will not *live beneath* the excellence of her dignity and ex-
istence whether it's dementia, a family member or anything
else.

Fin.

Epilogue

The only items that are celebrated when they turn old in the United States is wine, alcohol and money! Ok, so what about the importance of people? We watch when people turn 100, but not everyone is blessed to do this with grace and dignity. Some things we bring upon ourselves with diet and exercise behaviors, but other things could be the environment and culture in which we live or the dynamics of relationships. These factors played heavily in her diagnosis.

Mom is still with us, alive and kicking! This is a journey that takes one day at a time and should not be done alone--it must be supported. It is not easy and I can't do it by myself, and I know that. There are good days and frustrating days, but that's life. What hurts is watching the progression of what used to be. Dementia is not a normal progression of aging, but I believe that we are too comfortable in accepting it instead of finding out what must be done to defeat it. It is too prevalent in this society for my taste and that's why I am writing. *Something is wrong.*

Whatever the decision, I won't feel guilty in doing what is best for her or my immediate family. The point is to make it together. It is a time of flexibility and consideration, as it should be. Honor your parents, even if you don't understand decisions that were made, if they did everything for you, or did nothing for you. Still give them honor as the Word says to do and obey God. In the words of one of my dearest aunts, "He will make it alright in the end."

Talk Amongst Yourselves

Here are some questions and/or discussion starters for conversations with relatives, friends, book clubs, and so forth listed below. The order listed does not indicate importance:

1) Do you have a will? Do you know how you can get one done online or with an attorney?

2) Do you have any life insurance policies? If not, why? If so, are there beneficiaries mentioned?

3) Do your loved ones know about the policies and where they are if something happens to you?

4) What is Probate court and its function? Do you know the probate laws in your particular state and how they could affect you or someone else you lose?

5) Do you have a safe or a protected place where your "important papers" are kept?

6) Are your important papers or other bills updated if you or your loved one have undergone a name change, divorce, death, marriage, remarriage, blend-

ed family, sickness, cognitive disease?

7) Is your lifestyle working for you? How is your health? What about your mental, emotional and spiritual status?

8) Yes, please pray, seek God and wise counsel...however, if needed...GOING TO SEE A COUNSELOR OR THERAPIST DOES NOT MAKE YOU WEAK!

(Yes! I meant to yell and I hope you heard me--with love--it's all love!)

9) If you are a caregiver, accept help. There is help out there. Take care of yourself, please. You are not a martyr.

10) Are you in forgiveness mode? If not, ask the questions you need to ask, pray the prayers you need to pray, and have the needed truthful conversations in order to try to get there.

11) Does your diet and exercise reveal that you are trying to honor your body?

12) When my mother was diagnosed, the neurologist wanted her on a Mediterranean diet. Period. Check it out. It's healthy and pretty yummy too!

13) Do you know the Alzheimer's Association and what they do? Do you know where they are located?

14) Do you know how you can help seniors on a limited budget or maybe no resources? Contact the Adult Protective Services Offices in your state. They have people who will go check on your loved one and report back to you. They are also a great resource for help!!

Okay now...talk amongst yourselves...*please!*

Works Cited

1) Alzheimer's Association | Alzheimer's Disease & Dementia Help

   https://www.alz.org/

2) Alzheimer's Foundation of America

   https://alzfdn.org

3) Picture of Alzheimer's Disease

   (https://www.medicinenet.com/image-collection/ alzheimers_disease_picture/picture.htm)

www.ingramcontent.com/pod-product-compliance
Lightning Source LLC
Chambersburg PA
CBHW021153090426
42740CB00008B/1069